Release and Restoration

Release and Restoration

Thelma R. Hall & Loren Wilson Hall

EDITED AND WITH AN INTRODUCTION BY
Carmen Acevedo Butcher

Shorter College Press
Rome, Georgia

For information, contact
Shorter College Press
315 Shorter Avenue
Rome, Georgia 30165
Telephone 706.291.2121

Jacket & Interior Design by
Desktop Miracles, Inc., Stowe, Vermont
Publishing project management by Dr. Ross West
of Positive Difference Communications, Rome, Georgia

Publisher's Cataloguing-in-Publication

Hall, Thelma R. and Loren Wilson Hall
    Release and Restoration / by Thelma R. Hall and
Loren Wilson Hall.—1st ed.
    Edited and with an introduction by Carmen Acevedo
Butcher
        p.   cm.
    ISBN: 0-9662255-1-1
    1. Grief (Psychology)—Poetry.   2. Joy—Poetry.
3. Cancer—Poetry.   4. Love—Poetry.   5. Nature—
Poetry.   I. Title
PS

First edition: April 2004

Library of Congress Catalog Card Number: 2003116622

*To All Who Have Looked
into the Face of the Joker*

Contents

RELEASE AND RESTORATION

POEMS BY
Wilson Hall
⤞⤝

⤞⤝

Foreword

"Poet, mentor, professor, confidant, close friend...

"I loved sitting in Thelma's office. She always graciously moved from behind her desk to a closer chair so that we could chat. Even when I was a student here, sometimes we would spend at least an hour talking about anything—a poem, a memory, a problem, a class—anything.

"My sophomore year at Shorter, I decided to be an English major while taking Thelma's World Literature 203 class. I knew from the first lecture that Thelma loved not only literature but also life. Through her lectures, I knew that she understood life in ways that many people did not, and I also knew that I wanted to be just like her.

"She taught me that the best things in life happen unexpectedly—a poem while you're driving down the road, a career from a sophomore literature class, and a friendship from a simple conversation or a smile."

JENNIFER KELLOGG SIKES
ROME, GEORGIA

[*Editor's note*: Jennifer Kellogg Sikes, Assistant Professor of English at Shorter College in Rome, Georgia, is also a 1997 graduate of Shorter, and was one of Dr. Thelma Hall's students. Her reflections were featured on the front cover of the *Shorter Magazine*, Volume 127, Number 1.]

Introduction

Release and Restoration is a brave woman's dialogue with bad news. It is also a love story, as we will see, as well as a celebration of beauty. Dr. Thelma R. Hall spent the last five years of her life giving poetry readings, and traveling, teaching, and singing her way through a war with colon cancer, interrupted only by the overwhelming strength of leukemia in the spring of 2002. Her resilience still sings in the works she left behind.

> Sometimes certainty
> Spawns a complacent spirit
> Joy finds birth in doubt

One bright blue September day on the Shorter College campus that same year, I was peering at my computer screen when the mellow voice of Dr. Wilson Hall, Thelma's husband, boomed behind me, "Have you got 'September 11'? Sam Baltzer wants it now for a memorial service downtown this weekend."

We searched Thelma Hall's old computer (which I now use), but had no luck.

"Do you know how many unpublished poems Thelma left?"

"No."

"You should get them together and publish them, Wilson."

"Well, funny you should say that. John Ratledge and I were discussing this very same topic two days ago."

Wilson Hall left my office that day in an unaccustomed rush to find "September 11, 2001." He tossed behind him as he went, "Don't worry. I'll run home. I've got a hard copy there somewhere."

But I did worry. And that is how this book began. At first I focused on preserving Thelma's every unpublished work. To this end, Wilson brought me—off a desk here or a table there—the pieces Thelma left behind. I used seventeen of these. Only one seemed unfinished.

Thelma's last poems arrived in an unassuming manila folder, and as soon as Wilson handed them to me, I read them straight through. Then I turned back to the first poem and began again— only this time my hands rearranged the works unconsciously as I read, and all the while I was praying, *I hope this will please Thelma well.* During this process, her last poems danced into an organic wholeness, as a courageous theme emerged.

I selected the title, *Release and Restoration*, to reflect aspects of this theme. It is taken from two of the book's poems. *Release* originates in the Latin word, *relaxare*, meaning "to relax," and *restoration* derives from the Latin *restaurare*, "to renew, rebuild." During Thelma Hall's frightening, painful years living with the reality of metaports, weariness, scalpels, shots, chemotherapy, waiting, weakness, hair loss, and hard hospital beds, she found release and restoration in her old ally, poetry-making, and in the warmth of love. The poems also speak to the renewing power of beauty and finally to the ultimate release and restoration that is the mystery we call "death."

I was protecting the poignant shape Thelma's seventeen poems create together, when I realized there might be other poems still undiscovered. Wilson suggested I see Dr. John Ratledge, then Conductor of the Shorter College Chorale. John directed Thelma in the Chorale's productions at home and abroad, and he and Thelma developed a lively camaraderie. They exchanged poems for years in an informal creative dialogue. John's personal collection of Thelma's poems provided me with some new, important pieces: the poems quoted in this introduction, as well as "Self-Portrait," "Lost," and "I Walk My Childhood Once Again."

John's collection also showed me the artist at work. Yellow Post-it® notes that Thelma stuck on certain poems helped me understand her writing technique better. Wilson told me that Thelma wrote poetry (and even prose) the way a Chinese calligrapher paints. She turned the piece over in her mind for a long while, like a Chinese calligrapher standing staring at the canvas, and when she wrote the poem down—here he made the swift, concise motions of a calligrapher with ink on a brush—it was done, except for minor revisions.

I have the sense that if Thelma found herself making major revisions to what she envisioned as a poem, the piece was probably not working out; however, she did on occasion jot down prose accounts of experiences that moved her so that she could come back to them later, flipping through her notebook to see, as Wilson explained, if something in it "attracted her" to write a poem. On one yellow Post-it® note attached to "Release," Thelma Hall says, "These ['Release,' 'Restoration,' 'Fragmented Colors,' 'Wholeness,' 'I Have Wanted to Write a Poem,' 'The Joker,' and 'Communing with Snow'] are some poems I have been working on for a while—all before our heart-crushing experience of Sept. 11. Those [September 11 poems] are coming out as prose/poems right now, which probably means they have not yet 'jelled' into their place." I never found these "prose/poems" dealing with September 11th, 2001, but I can imagine her keeping an image from one, a line from another, combining their best features into the beautifully polished lyric, "September 11, 2001."

Significantly, seven of the poems Thelma gave John are duplicates of ones in Wilson's manila folder. These seven shared poems are as follows: "Fragmented Colors," "Wholeness," "I Have Wanted to Write a Poem," "Release," "Restoration," "The Joker," and "Communing with Snow." They are the ballast of this book. Wilson said,

"When all this started five years ago, John told Thelma, 'You must write about it.'" He meant her cancer.

Obviously she did, but she never acknowledged that fact. Perhaps the poems were too close to her struggle with cancer—perhaps she could not bring herself to admit the bad news they contain. Instead, Wilson called me one day to say he had remembered what kind of book Thelma was working on at the time of her death—she was fashioning a second book of poems about China. (Thelma published a chapbook, *Among Chinese*, in 1998.) I e-mailed Wilson, "Where are these other Chinese poems then?" and he e-mailed back:

> I do not know that Thelma had gotten far along enough to settle on a theme for the "Yantai Summer Rain" collection, although she was sure that the poem by that name would be in the book and be the title of the book. My sense was that she was collecting poems that would show the lovability of the Chinese people and their profound humanness. That was what most attracted her to them and what she tried hardest to express in her poems about them.

Literally a handful of these poems did turn up later. Of these, "Yantai Summer Rain" was selected. The other four Chinese poems were not included because they fall outside the scope of this book, and also because they are not quite still enough. I did not wish to dilute *Release and Restoration*'s strength.

The eponymic poem of Thelma's unfinished "Yantai Summer Rain" collection intimates that Thelma found strength in simplicity—in the loveliness of rain and in the "comfortable awareness of the present moment" that a new land's unusual culture often fosters in the traveler. The obviously delightful foreign land in "Yantai Summer Rain" is China, where Thelma and Wilson enjoyed teaching four summers. Ironically, though, what a forbidding and alien country Cancer certainly is, yet within its restricted borders, Thelma also found unending sustenance in the timeless beauty of Now.

Stanza IV of a larger unfinished poem called "Snow Scenes" shows this grace. Small beauties are nourishing:

I can turn my face toward Mecca
but Fujiyama is too hard to climb.
I have slipped from ice
and plunged headlong
into crevasses where snows
choked and smothered me.
Why should I scale such heights
when the small yellow flower
growing at its base
has all it needs to flourish
and all it needs to die.

When Wilson Hall proofed the initial editing of Thelma's final poems, he said, "I am satisfied with your sense of the theme—'a brave woman's dialogue with bad news.' That's a wonderful first line, for that is what it was. It is a theme that [Thelma] would not have thought to select for herself, but it is the truest theme of the poems." He also noted that "Houses Have Wombs" and "Houses Also Have Minds"—two of the works he had found and given to me—are older poems, for they were typed on a typewriter rather than on a computer.

Thelma's last poems are brief, but their message is long. *Release and Restoration* tenders twenty songs daring the "dark nights" described in Gail Tremblay's poem, "It is Important,"* which Thelma typed up and gave to John Ratledge not long before she died—"[T]his is the poem I told you about. I know you will appreciate it. It is said to evoke Native American mythology, but I love it for its specificity of thought." The poem's first six lines evoke the way Thelma Hall lived, and the way she loved life:

* Gail Tremblay, *Indian Singing: Poems*, rev. ed. (Corvallis, Oregon: Calyx Books, 1998), 22.

On dark nights, when thoughts fly like nightbirds
looking for prey, it is important to remember
to bless with names every creature that comes
to mind, to sing a thankful song and hold
the magic of the whole creation close in the heart,
to watch light dance and know the sacred is alive.

A key element of Thelma's ability "to bless" was her husband
of forty-five years, Wilson Hall, and his understanding of beauty,
as seen in her poems, "Communing with Snow" and "Fragmented
Colors," and in his poems, "The Handprint," "Like Being Under an
Overturned Bowl," and "When I Die." Thelma tells him in "The way,"
"[Y]ou listen, always, . . . / you center my life but make sure / I'm not
held too tightly to the moorings." So this book is also a love story.
Thelma dedicated her *Sunlight and Stones* to Wilson Hall, "whose
warmth and love sustain me." She would have been pleased to know
her husband was asked to read her poem, "The way," at the summer
2002 wedding of Jennifer Kellogg and Brian Sikes. The poem's celebration of a love as cozy as "the old robe / and sweat suit we put on /
as soon as we are home" is richly epithalamic, and its location at the
heart of this volume is certainly significant.

Thelma Hall's poem, "Lost," shows that life and love exist even
in the face of death. It speaks to the strange roads of a terminal ill-
ness, where "no landmark is familiar," "memory sings off-key," and
"[h]armony is not expected," but the poet also finds a strange joy in
this place, even, one could say, a freedom: "I have no destination; I
am not / expected anywhere"; she says her mind "slips away from
routines." For Thelma, these would have included the administrative
routines and professorial routines she juggled cheerfully for many
years as Chair of the Division of Humanities and Professor of English. Against this background, "Lost" describes her new and unusual
freedom—harmony is not only "not expected," but also, Thelma
adds, "not desired," and the last line of the poem achieves a sort of

Keatsian "negative capability" as the poet exults "in the discordant, unmatched / remnants of myself, lost / but free."

"Lost," as title, is also a love story in itself. Perhaps it reflects a moment of romantic paronomasia in the middle of Thelma's crisis with cancer. Wilson's first name is Loren, meaning "lost." *Lost*, in turn, derives from the Latin word, *luere*, "to atone for"—literally, "to become at one with"—connoting harmony and loyalty. But Thelma knew *lost* also derives from the Greek *lyein*, for "to loosen, dissolve, destroy." This poem reflects both of these notions; because her fragile and fragmented spirit rests in her husband's abiding devotion, Thelma is, as the last word says, "free," even as her old strong and comfortable self is steadily destroyed by cancer. I know from phone conversations with Thelma what a steady hand Wilson was during her illnesses.

The last eighteen poems of this volume are eloquent in their testimony to this great and enduring love. They are achingly articulate. Wilson wrote most of them as a spontaneous reaction to the loss of Thelma. Of these eighteen poems, one requires some explanation. "Standing above Your Grave" deals with, Wilson says, the funeral of "a dear friend of mine in my early days at Shorter." In his November 12, 2002, lecture, "Poetry as a Means of Exploring the Self," delivered at Shorter College, Wilson remembers the friend he lost those many years ago:

> I had come to enjoy my morning conversations with him in the coffee lounge, and so I was shocked and saddened when word came that he had died. His funeral was in the cold depths of December, one of those days when the sky is blue and clear, the light is bright and the temperature just above freezing. The insight, that things are well in death, came in the form of a bird flying.

Release and Restoration is a duet sung over the fence of death, by a husband and a wife, to each other, and to the world, about love and beauty and bereavement. And, although Thelma starts singing first, Wilson soon follows; their individual voices blend, as they do in the sweetest duets, becoming one as we read, and then read again. Themes and words (like *lost, beauty, rain*, and *music*) echo. Together Thelma and Wilson praise this world's loveliness, and together they face death. The authorship of the individual poems is indicated in the table of contents and also with a minimum of interruption before each of the two sections by a page naming "Thelma Hall" and the other, "Wilson Hall."

The ironic tone of Thelma Hall's poem, "The Wall," deserves special notice. It is positioned right after the initial poem in this book because of its irony. I believe this is the bitter existence Thelma had every right to choose, and in fact looked square in the face, but rejected. Adamantly.

As a former student of both Thelma and Wilson Hall, I have experienced a special happiness editing this book of their poems. I thank Wilson, John Ratledge, and Jennifer Kellogg Sikes for their openness. Special appreciation goes to Mr. Gary Davis, Shorter's Postmaster, and to Mr. Jerry Wiley, Assistant Postmaster (and Copy-Meister), who *always* exceed my expectations. Dr. Sam Baltzer, Professor of Music across the campus from me, unwittingly sparked this book by his initial request for one of Thelma's poems. Doris Griffin Acevedo provided expert editing, as usual. April Baeza helped with typing. With an aptitude for administrative organizing that belies her equally excellent scholarly skills, Dr. Kasee Clifton Laster, our new Chair of Humanities, made our year of transition an exceptionally smooth one. Thanks also to Dr. William H. "Bill" Rice, the Dean of the School for Liberal Arts, for his encouragement and help during the initial publishing stage of this book, and to Mr. Bruce Watterson, Associate Vice President of Institutional Relations at Shorter College, for his savvy way of creating sincere public relations masterpieces. Shorter College's President, Dr. Ed L. Schrader; Provost, Dr. Harold Newman; and CFO, Mr. Wayne

Dempsey, have given outstanding advice and support. Andrea Hollander Budy, whose *House Without a Dreamer* won the 1993 Nicholas Roerich Poetry Prize, read the manuscript with great care, and it benefited from her kind, perceptive spirit. Finally, Dr. Ross West deserves the most attentive gratitude for his high standards and publishing acumen.

These poems have been a joy to edit. Thelma left her manuscripts in impeccable order, despite her departure in medias res, and Wilson Hall's poems were edited first, some of them, in the old-fashioned manner of being allowed to steep quietly in a drawer for years, and the other, more recent creations, were polished via the magic of e-mail while Dr. Hall was teaching in Salzburg. It cost me very little indeed to insert a few hyphens in Thelma's work or to correct a few spellings in Wilson's; however, I would have much preferred the happy duty of proofreading a retyped manuscript that Thelma herself had handed me, Wilson by her side.

CARMEN ACEVEDO BUTCHER
JUNE 17, 2003
ROME, GEORGIA

Thelma Hall

SELF-PORTRAIT

A bare, aging tree
Etches its lacy black face
On a winter sky

THE WALL

I have erected a wall
against all hurtful things.
No floods of anguish
can even dampen this sanctuary.
Being soundproof,
nothing screams or crashes,
or if it does, it only quivers
in helpless vibration
against the opaque hardness.
But safely isolated
in idyllic capsule,
the hurt of loneliness
floods and beats vainly
against the interior wall.
Somewhere yellow wings
stroke the sky in delicate whirls,
and laughter skips and tumbles
through the wind and sun,
but the wall, being firm
and not capricious,
holds.

September 11, 2001

How can we speak of it, what words
can describe a reality we do not,
cannot recognize?
We watched one plane, then two,
crash against giants of steel and glass.
They looked so small, like wasps
stinging two great steeds.
We watched, horrified, as this small
impact spread, imploding
these symbols of strength so that
they folded in upon themselves
and crumbled before our eyes.
We could not allow ourselves
to think what fell besides
the melted steel, what great
gaping holes would open in our hearts,
how we, too, would feel the dark,
inward sinking, how the blackening
smoke, dust, and debris would keep
their chokehold on our very souls.
Debris was meant to be brick
and stone and steel, throwaway trash
we no longer need, not, oh surely not,
this fragile flesh of thousands,
so completely, utterly, gone.

While the smoke still rose
from the smoldering mass, we watched
the human spirit rise like the phoenix
from its ashes, felt the need to love
and be loved, felt around our bodies
the strong supporting arms as one
after another, strong men, exhausted,
torn apart by grief, clasped one another
and held on tightly, then returned
to the task at hand, determined
to rescue someone, anyone,
and keep hope, at least, alive.

In Central Park, butterflies still
flew from flower to flower and
water ran smooth and free
from lakes and fountains.

Three days later, bells rang
from cathedrals, children played
in parks, weddings and prayers,
candles and flags, singing and praise
began the healing, as real as sunlight
glistening through green trees,
as palpable as grief, as glorious
as hope.
Halleluyah, Alleluja, Hallelouia
Amen.

Fragmented Colors

We watched the sunset,
painfully beautiful,
after hearing news that shattered
our world into broken fragments
of grays and blacks.
Before disease made us fragile
and helpless, nothing
could have diminished our deep trust
that beauty, symbol of the good
that made life worthwhile, endured,
even drove the darkness
to hidden coves where only
the weak and insensitive dwelled.
And even now, though we look out
from a dark place, the spangled sky
throws fragments of color
into the deep recesses
of these stone walls.

WHOLENESS

Something has stolen away
some important part of me.
I awake at night and lie there
wondering what is gone, and
unable to know what is gone,
I cannot retrieve it.
Or sometimes in brightest sunlight
with shadows dancing so alive
through the brilliance of summer green,
I feel that absence of something.
When I speak, I wonder whether
I sound the same or whether I am
mimicking the person I once was.
In the worst of these moments,
I feel the theft so keenly
I can almost see the sneering face
and glaring eyes of my abductor
and feel the pain of being dragged
through mud and debris and the
suffocation of being hidden
in some dark cave.
Then, no amount of sunlight
dancing through trees
can bring back the joy of wholeness.

But then, some inner strength
comes back to remind me
that perhaps the part of me
carried away was my lesser self,
the part that held me tied
too close to flesh,
and I can wait then for the light
to creep into all the corners
and reveal that no part of me
lies crouched and abandoned
in despair.

I Have Wanted to Write a Poem

I have wanted to write a poem
to go down deep
to where the spirit lies,
but I am too conscious of my body.
Since the first snip of flesh
said something lived inside me
that must be destroyed,
since the long track of the knife
opened my body for this removal
then clamped me back together
leaving a glaring scar,
since the radiation blazoned
into my body an angry force,
and chemo sent its love poison
coursing through my blood,
I have wanted to write a poem,
but I am still too conscious
of my body and too afraid
that the spirit might be
too far away to reach.

RELEASE

Wolves howled in the night,
a low, mournful sound
like crying.
Snow covered my tracks
as I stepped out from white,
sterile halls which had helped me
lock up death in a deep black
coffin.
I gathered their sounds
to my breast. Their wet fur
touched my face, and in the night
filled with the coldest stars,
we howled together.
In the morning,
when the first light scared away
the wolves,
I went back to my bed,
fastened my legs back down
in their warm restraints
so that blood would flow freely
and choked down the last
warm, furry howl.
No one ever knew I had been gone.

As my wounds slowly healed,
the night sounds faded
far deeper than I could track,
yet I still longed for
release,
secretly hoping the wolves
would return.

Restoration

When the alien that wrapped
its fingers into my flesh
let loose its grip, turned friendly,
emotions changed like budded flowers
under time-lapse magic.
Before, they had bloomed
on rocky cliffs, clinging to moss,
and though they had beckoned for me
to lean far out to touch them,
the edge was a jagged razor
that cut my hope.
Now, red and vibrant, yellow as sunlight,
they bloom in window boxes, swell
wild and random on river banks,
assert themselves through fallen leaves,
Yet still, I stroke, not pick, their
fragile blooms.

HOUSES HAVE WOMBS

I know because I have curled
down into several warm, quiet places
in the dim, misty haze of memory.

Now, having been sent forth,
I try to discover them again.
I sit awhile in each, suspended,
floating, not completely loose,
yet not really attached.
Which one is home? What do they mean,
these walls and nails,
these carefully positioned,
partitioned rooms?

Sometimes I push walls down
and reshape the spaces.
Why not triangles? or circles
would be nice.
Other times I am soothed
by the bars that lock me into
tiny spaces where adventure
is impossible and nothing is
expected.

HOUSES ALSO HAVE MINDS

They can plot against you,
gently lead you astray,
seduce you, leave you wandering
like a wanton ghost
along the exterior walls,
looking for windows,
but finding none.

What if a house, having a mind
decided to cast me out?
Where would I go?
Walls are not always prisons.
When you reach out to feel your way
along a wall and down or up a stair,
it's not so bad if you lose your way.
There will be another wall, a stair
to climb or descend, even if you
don't know where they lead.
But a hand reached out in air,
well, that's something else
altogether.

If there is no wall to touch,
you feel like a drowning person
must feel knowing desperate hands
are sweeping through murky water
but just missing every time,
or like the person floating
through the air the moment before
the earth looms up, a green mass
but no cushion for the fall.

THE WAY

the pink glow of sunrise
spills over the lawn and peers
into our bedroom window—
the way our house feels, wrapped
around us like the old robe
and sweat suit we put on
as soon as we are home,
comforted by a cup of tea and
the familiar sound of a teaspoon
tinkling against the sides of the cup—
the way our black and white cat
sits high on the bank behind our house
keeping watch or surveying her place
or merely testing the wind that gently
turns her fur into a soft, quivering fan—
the way you sit asleep in our reclining chair,
relaxed, at peace—
the way you listen, always, as I tell
about some happening or passage
from a book, forgiving my jumping
from point to point, my impatience
to race ahead in a story, my forgetting
beginnings, confusing middles, my
remembering only bright spots
or moments of grief—

the way you center my life but make sure
I'm not held too tightly to the moorings,
assuring me that this is the way
that moves, with grace, through love.

THE JOKER

He sat on a gray stone wall, smiling.
"I knew you would come," he said
to all who passed.
"You'll know your fate
by the changes in my face."
Never one to ponder fate
or fear the future, I watched
as his features gleamed like sunlight
or glowered like broken dreams.
Then boldly, I faced him and trembled
as his eyes turned red and his face
grew ashy white. I couldn't speak,
and he did not need words
to tell me my life would be
forever changed.

WAKING IN FEAR

Thunder rumbled and lightning
cut orange streaks
across her tulle curtains.
My mother, startled, called out
to me, a daughter never
confident in storms.
When I reached her, she held out her hand.
Her unseeing eyes were dark pools,
aware only of a flashing glare.
When she said, "Would you stay with me?"
I lay down beside her and pulled up the quilt
she had made years before, matching
carefully colors and patterns.
I put my arm around her tiny body,
the way she had held me as a small child.
Hearing her stomach growl,
I got up and brought back a glass of milk.
When the storm subsided,
I returned to my own bed, proud
that I had satisfied both her fear and her hunger.
I awoke, fearful, not from streaks of lightning
threatening, but from having dreamed
that I was blind, and from the emptiness
I had felt when I reached out for the
absent child beside me.

Only now do I realize
how small a part of her fear and hunger
I could understand.

COMMUNING WITH SNOW

When the soft snow began to fall
in late November, as unexpected
as a daisy in winter, it fell
in white spangles from all sides
of our new garden room.
You turned to me as we started
to church and said, "You go ahead
to sing in the choir, but I must
stay here to watch the snow.
It won't last very long."
I saw its soft, powdery surface
barely clinging to the ground
and wondered whether it would
last until I returned.

In church, the stained glass windows
shut out the snow, and except
for the muted light that dimmed
the colors from the inside,
the world outside was lost to view.
Words rose and fell, dropping
softly into hushed silence, and
music lingered like mist that
clings to the skin even after
the sun appears to dispel the rain.

When I returned, I knew that you
had been one with the snow,
had been with it in reveries
of slow-moving canoes and
campfires built to still the cold
of late November's jeweled surprise.
It did not matter that the ground
was already almost bare again
or that the sky had lightened
and blue streaked through the
sprinkled treetops,
You were at peace with a gift
of grace—a morning touched with
silence deeper than words or music.

YANTAI SUMMER RAIN

Today, with some of my students,
I tromped through rain, stomping
Chinese puddles into rivulets
with my Reebok boats.
The wind fought hard against my umbrella,
a weak, pitiful thing, no match
for the decisive wind.
I held its tip end like a man pulling his hat
to prevent its flying away.
For two hours my body was cooled by clothes
that clung damp to my skin.
I reveled in the coolness after 100 degree heat.
During this time, we talked of poets
angry with their fathers yet loving
even the hurt they had brought them.
They did not remember surface things
but longed instead for deep memory,
a spiritual union.
We forgot our wet clothes,
our bedraggled wind-blown hair,
our need for approval, as we read aloud,
searching the words for meanings
deep beneath the surface sounds.
But we received mainly a comfortable
awareness of the present moment.

Two hours later, the rain had ceased,
and the water slowly receded from the streets.
Deep-throated tree frogs croaked
their pleasure to the twisting wind.
Back in the apartment, I stripped off
the outer layer and hung it up to dry,
knowing that what had seeped inside
would continue to feed the trickling well.

Running Through the Dark

I run, feet pounding the cobblestoned street.
The dark night engulfs me.
Where I have been is a deeper darkness
where dreams clamped around me,
coffin-like until I awoke,
panic suffocating me, sweat
dampening my clothes.

I run past trees full of resting black birds.
They do not stir from my heavy breathing
or seem aware of me at all.
An owl's bright eyes seek my face,
but it does not call my name.
This should be a sign, I think,
that the darkness does not want me here.

I run, my shadow following me,
and beams of light streak through the trees.
Somewhere ahead the source of light
awaits me. All I have to do is run
until the darkness fades away.

Restoring Houses

They pull the roof, center beam,
splintered walls
back down.
They land off-center, but perhaps
will stand.
Determined to reshape, reform,
they put together pieces of rooms,
plug holes, cover scars with paint.

They kneel to collect the fallen nails,
woodchips, tools
and hold their breath, waiting
for the angers to wrench loose the boards.

"First the sacrifice, then the restoration,"
they say, unable to know
why walls chip and crumble—
the irony of repair.

BATTLING THE ELEMENTS

You can sandbag the door,
nail crossing bars over windows,
prop up the roof with steel
and anchor the floor in cement,
but just as you settle
into acceptance of creaks
and thumps and moaning wind,
under the doorway will creep
the subtlest of memories
to startle and shake the peace.
It comes in the night
in the shape of dreams,
in the middle of sun-bright thoughts
of hope and love.
Sometimes, determined to invade,
it rattles the protective bars,
floods and threatens to drown,
then coats the survivor
with mud and debris.
It bends and breaks
or warps, at least,
all foundations.

What is it that says
"Build again, this time
on higher ground
or snug under a mountain's shadow,"
and we listen and begin anew.

LOST

I hold the car steady
around curving, narrow roads.
I have no destination; I am not
expected anywhere;
no landmark is familiar.
Sparrows flit among the trees,
and light jumps from tree limb to tree limb
before sprinkling the ground,
playful among fallen leaves.
My mind slips away from routines
and fragments into smooth, uneven particles,
not hard like stones
nor bright like sunlight
dancing among the leaves
but secure in a peaceful
randomness.
In the place I left behind,
familiarity chiseled identity
into stone.
Here, memory sings off-key,
casting a haze of scattered thoughts
that hang like Spanish moss
from massive, sheltering trees.
One small breeze shakes a fragile thought
but cannot dislodge it.
Harmony is not expected, not desired.

A symphony demands attention,
a wholeness too difficult to attain
as delicate, disconnected threads
struggle to weave themselves
into oneness.
I exult in the discordant, unmatched
remnants of myself, lost
but free.

I Walk My Childhood
Once Again

In the sizzling sweet honeysuckle days
when even flies rest in shadows
and bare feet seek the underside
of freshly plowed soil
or push deeply into the leaf-mole thickness
of the winter-floored woods,
I walk my childhood once again.

I walk the paths down rocky cliffs
to the whispered coolness and freedom
of the winding creek, and when there,
I lie, legs dangling,
like a prone and backward L,
upon a gently sloping stone
and pour my daydreams
like libations into the water.

I walk the hard-packed, earth-brown roads
to somewhere and someone
whose reality has now faded—
before the time of philosophical retrospect,
before distance and directions
were suspended by a question mark,
when roads were for walking
and not for symbolic abstraction.

And though I walk with this child
who has since selved into many,
this earth-joined, sun-baked one self
remains distinct, a core
for the many vacillating fragments.
And so I walk my childhood once again,
for all paths lead back home.

Wilson Hall

BEFORE EPIPHANY

Beneath dark approaching storm clouds
Under dense, overhanging river birches
The daylight is muted, diffused, sourceless
The air like polarized glass.
Mist hangs low over the river
Dense along the surface.
Smells of jasmine, methane, lush greenness
Thicken in the air.
Shadowless, lusterless banks of green
Of yellow root, muscadine, ferns, and hemlock
Drape the river shore.
All hang timeless, motionless, waiting.
First comes the shower of yellow leaves
Then come the first large drops.

SOMETIMES IN THE NIGHT

Sometimes when I awaken in the night
I forget that I am old
And reach for you under the cover
and more awake
Hold you close and remember.

Sometimes when I awaken in the night
My mind has jumped ahead
To a future blackness, and I am alone in bed.
Then I reach for you under the cover
And finding you
Fix my hand just so on your hip.
Comforted, I sleep again.

Sometimes when I awaken in the night
I feel your hand on my shoulder
Then on my ribs and waist, and come to rest there
And I know what you think.

Do You Remember

Do you remember
We almost missed the sign?

But we saw it
A very small blue arrow
Pointing down a dirt road
And the word *Restaurant*
Written on its shaft.

So, even though it was three o'clock
In the afternoon
We made the almost U-turn
And eased down the hill to the veranda
Of a building that looked out and over
A deep, Black Forest valley that held
Tiny sheep and a tiny tractor, tiny houses
And a yellow, thread-like continuation of the road.
We ordered tea and cheesecake
That was not made on this earth.

Across the road the gray sheep grazed
Under a brilliant, spring-blue sky
And far away down the slope a cow's bell klonked
And klonked in the mid-afternoon air.
And you cried because it was all so beautiful.

And then afterward came the leukemia
And this day became a stay against
What was to come.

MAD ANNIE'S PRAYER

I cannot pray for my pain's relief
And Preacher, you cannot,
If God does not relieve the pain of all.

Why should I be chosen?

If pain must be
And there is no escape
Let me, Oh God, assume all pain
All kinds of pain of all the people
And make pain my carriage out of this world.
Trailing clouds of pain would I go, to God who is my home.
I pray for that
And Preacher, you can, too.

As the Hawk Does the Wind

I have watched the red tail turn
High above mountains, rising in thermals.
I have watched him sail down the wind
Planing in speed, diving to flare, stall, and lift again.
He feels the wind in his wings
And lives by the realness of a thing not seen.

Oh that I could rise in God's grace, bank and sail
As the hawk does the wind,
Could lean on unseenness with sureness
As the hawk does the wind.

COMPLETE

If it is a cold, November afternoon
And I am walking across the campus
Under dark branches of bare maples
And leafless red oak trees

If when I stop to watch the last light
Of day melt into the gray clouds
Beyond the lighted cityscape
And pull my coat together

If then you are beside me
A palpable feminine presence
In realness or in memory
The day dies complete.

EVERY MORNING
WHEN I MAKE TEA

For Thelma

Every morning when I make tea
I remember a tiny Black Forest village
Deep in a narrow, steep-sided gorge
Where we wandered the streets alone.

Rising mists hang in the Tannenbaum tops
Dissolving upward into low, gray sky.
Streets glisten in the wetness of the early May morning
And you are always laughing
From under the red hood of your rain parka,
Your eyes glistening, too, in the heavy, wet air.

Pretending not to be American tourists
We speak German.
Strolling through the wood-carving shop
And the art gallery and the bakery
We are the only customers.

In the teashop we buy a hundred grams
Of *Ostfriesische Mischung*.
At noon we lunch with the local forest workers,
Secretaries, lawyers, and shop girls
In a side-street café smelling of potato soup
And cooked onions, fresh bread, and pork roast.
Here German language and laughter swirl about us
Like water around fish.

As water drops from the eaves outside our window
I hold your hand across the table
Waiting for food.

All of that still resides in the aroma of tea.

I Lit a Candle, Dear, Today

I lit a candle, dear, today.
It burns in Nevski Dom*
A place you never were to see.
It sends up prayer for your peace and mine
In separate worlds, together

Just as chorale music lifts and echoes
In the cathedral's vaults and chambers
Dying away softly to God's ear.

The thing that divides us
Is not a wall, not a valley, not a river
Not even an interface between two worlds.

The division is but the limit of my knowing
The sum of my experience
The totality of my mind.

My ignorance spreads, thus, an illusion
Over the mystery of God
As insubstantial as reflection on water.

---

* *Dom* is a German word for *Cathedral*.
Nevski Cathedral is in Sofia, Bulgaria.

From your side
Where no earthly limit is
Nothing is between us.
Only transition
Without break or interruption.

I made a poem, dear, today
I made it in Nevski Dom
To pierce the dark
To lift a prayer
To cross a barrier that does not exist.

Far Away

Far away a piano holds a tune that I can scarcely hear.
I cannot distinguish the notes, one from another,
But the smooth flow of indistinct sound evokes in me

A melancholy

And reminds me of things that are no more:
Good friends, good times, laughter in your eyes.

ANGUISH

It's not that God spoke
And there was a flower.
It's that the flower
Is God speaking.

Oh God,
Speak her name again
Please.

STANDING ABOVE YOUR GRAVE

Standing above your grave
In the bitter December afternoon
My eyes held clear sunlight
Bright on the raw, newly exposed chert.
My mind pictured your face
Motionless within the cold, sun-washed box.
By your request there were no flowers.

From under the preacher's monotone
My eyes raised
Looking across the treeless, broad valley
Of cemetery, blank houses, and empty farms.
They followed the long flight
Of the afternoon's only bird
From a horizon in the east
Toward the west where the sun
Was winter bright.
Gray and voiceless it flew
And my heart leaped up.

Twenty years later
Under fallen leaves I found
Lost toys you cried for.

THE HANDPRINT

I've heard your awed and silent cry, Cousin,
  Across unnumbered centuries dim grown
  Your palm print poem soft in ochre blown
  Against the dull cave wall in Gargas' Glen.
    The self inside you leapt to be unfrozen
    To say, "I am" upon the timeless stone.
You left your mark of mind—not bone alone.
    I feel your fossil joy conveyed therein.

    It wasn't much to palm a wall and blow
    A silhouetted hand in dust outlined
    But that prime effort did on Man bestow
    The poet's mind, new and unrefined,
And cast the way that inward man must plod
Himself to light—to stand in the image of God.

LIKE BEING UNDER AN OVERTURNED BOWL

For Don Cornelius

Like being under an overturned bowl

The night sky above me black as tar
With a billion diamond-bright stars

Like some gigantic electronic game

And the moon just above the western horizon
A golden fingernail clipping

I standing on a crunching oyster bar
And the canoe stranded in two inches of low tide

The water world around me flat as a table
And black as the sky

I had no idea how to get around in the maze
Of shallow tide and exposed oyster racks
All the same shade of black

I had no idea how far away the marsh beach was

And I thought, how in hell can I tell anyone
How beautiful this is?

WHEN I DIE

When I die
I want to go and live in art.

I don't mean to live in Michaelangelo's *David*
Or the Sistine Chapel
Nor in some ancient art museum
No matter how famous or old or large the collection

But in the idea of art

As did my daughter once
When she was four and tied a small blanket around her neck
And, barefoot, announced that she was going to live in a palace.
And all afternoon she did
Flowing through the invisible rooms and halls
Eating its unseeable food
Talking to its incorporeal inhabitants.

So I, dead and incorporeal,
Will inhabit Strauss' *Death and Transfiguration*.
I will be in the thing that speaks to your heart
When the notes pour out like rain and wind.
I will move through the morning sunlight of
Friedrich's *Morgen im Riesengebirge*.
I will be in what rivets your attention
To the horizon and the cross.

I will live in the mood
Of Hardy's Egdon Heath
And in the haunting dusky voice of Roberta Flack.

I do not want to be physical again.
But unembodied and alive.

I want to live in the thing you do not see
When you see the sunset
But you know that something is there
In that thing you do not hear in the wind
But you know it just the same.

I want to live in—not beauty
Beauty's too abstract for me—
But in the thing you feel
When you finish *Song of Myself*
And lay the book aside.
In that moment that hangs
Between the last note of
Rachmaninoff's *Ave Maria*
And the first thought that must follow
I could spend an eternity.

I want to go and live in art
When I die.

The artist delights to go back to the first
Chaos of the world. . . . All is without form
and void. . . .

WILLIAM HAZLITT,
ESSAYIST, 1816

BEYOND THE DOOR OF OUR KNOWING

Lift up your heads, Oh ye gates
And be ye lifted up, ye everlasting doors
That the King of Glory shall come in.

Whence comes the King of Glory, that He comes through a gate?
Whence comes the King of Glory, that He comes through a door?

He comes from beyond the door of our knowing.
He comes from the land of our faith,
From the unarticulated Void, where all possibility exists.
He is Order that conquers the chaos.
He is the music that breaks from the noise.

Men go beyond the door
Out to the edge of knowing
To the place of all possibility.

They take their passions, and these become poems.
They take their joys, and these become music.
They take their griefs, and these become symphony.
They take their questions and resolve them in paint.
They take their longings and there they meet God.

Out there are the stem cells of creation
Where color becomes music
And music becomes stone,
Where word resolves into flesh.

So lift up your heads, Oh ye gates
And be ye lifted up, ye everlasting doors
That we may see the Creator.

BENEDICTION IN SMOKE

Let the smoke from our campfire rise in this valley.
Let it drift in thick haze over the morning bright river
Through the winter bare twigs of oak trees and hickories.
Let the morning sun strike it, white and rising.
Let it glisten and become incandescent.
Let the deer by the waterfall sniff it and start.
Let the birds fly over it, turn, and wonder at it.

It is our thanksgiving for what we are.

Let it say to the world that we stop here
That we breakfast here
And breathe the air and drink the water
But move on
Covering our fire site with leaves and duff
Leaving no mark that we came this way
But knowing in our hearts that we did.